AWESOME ANIMAL HEROES

CESAR
MILLAN

LAUREN KUKLA

Consulting Editor, Diane Craig, M.A./Reading Specialist

Super Sandcastle

An Imprint of Abdo Publishing
abdopublishing.com

abdopublishing.com

Published by Abdo Publishing, a division of ABDO, PO Box 398166, Minneapolis, Minnesota 55439. Copyright © 2017 by Abdo Consulting Group, Inc. International copyrights reserved in all countries. No part of this book may be reproduced in any form without written permission from the publisher. Super SandCastle™ is a trademark and logo of Abdo Publishing.

Printed in the United States of America, North Mankato, Minnesota
102016
012017

THIS BOOK CONTAINS RECYCLED MATERIALS

Editor: Paige Polinsky
Content Developer: Nancy Tuminelly
Cover and Interior Design and Production: Mighty Media, Inc.
Photo Credits: Allan Weissmann/Cesar's Way Inc., Allen Birnbach/Cesar's Way Inc., AP Images, Everett Collection NYC, Gary Brandon/Cesar's Way Inc., George Gomez/Cesar's Way Inc., Getty Images, Gio Alma/Cesar's Way Inc., Shutterstock, Stephanie Lynn Warga/Cesar's Way Inc.

Publisher's Cataloging-in-Publication Data

Names: Kukla, Lauren, author.
Title: Cesar Millan / by Lauren Kukla.
Description: Minneapolis, MN : Abdo Publishing, 2017. | Series: Awesome animal heroes
Identifiers: LCCN 2016944663 | ISBN 9781680784374 (lib. bdg.) | ISBN 9781680797909 (ebook)
Subjects: LCSH: Millan, Cesar, 1969- --Juvenile literature. | Animal specialists--Mexico--Biography--Juvenile literature. | Dogs--Training--Juvenile literature. | Dogs--Behavior--Juvenile literature. | Human-animal communication--Juvenile literature. | Animal behavior--Juvenile literature.
Classification: DDC 636.7 [B]--dc23
LC record available at http://lccn.loc.gov/2016944663

Super SandCastle™ books are created by a team of professional educators, reading specialists, and content developers around five essential components—phonemic awareness, phonics, vocabulary, text comprehension, and fluency—to assist young readers as they develop reading skills and strategies and increase their general knowledge. All books are written, reviewed, and leveled for guided reading, early reading intervention, and Accelerated Reader™ programs for use in shared, guided, and independent reading and writing activities to support a balanced approach to literacy instruction.

CONTENTS

THE DOG WHISPERER

Cesar Millan is a dog **behaviorist**. He often works with dogs that may be unsafe. He is called the Dog Whisperer. Millan stars in popular TV shows. He has also written dog training books. Some people don't agree with Millan's methods. But others think he has saved the lives of many dogs.

Cesar Millan

CESAR MILLAN

BORN: August 27, 1969, Culiacán, Sinaloa, Mexico

MARRIED: Ilusion Wilson (1994–2012)

CHILDREN: André Millan, Calvin Millan

DOG BOY

Cesar Millan was born César Felipe Millán Favela. He grew up on a farm in Sinaloa, Mexico. There, the farm dogs often followed Cesar around. When Cesar was five, his family moved to Mazatlán, Mexico. The children there called him *el perrero*. That is Spanish for "dog boy."

The Pacific coast of Mazatlán, Mexico

DREAMS
OF DOGS

Young Cesar dreamed of training dogs. He worked for a veterinarian. When Cesar was older, he tried to become a dog trainer. But jobs were hard to find. So in 1990, Cesar snuck into California.
He didn't speak English. But he was ready for a new life.

As a child, Cesar loved the TV show Lassie. *It starred a heroic dog.*

Cesar had no money when he arrived in San Diego, California.

A DREAM COME TRUE

Millan eventually found work as a pet **groomer**. Later he became a dog walker. In 1998, Millan opened the Dog **Psychology** Center (DPC). The center worked with dogs that needed training.

Millan worked well with dogs that were angry or scared.

Millan worked with the dogs of famous sports and movie stars. Basketball player Dennis Rodman and actress Jada Pinkett-Smith were two of his clients.

FINDING FAME

In 2002, a newspaper wrote about Millan's work. Soon after, he was offered a TV show. *The Dog Whisperer* first aired in 2004 on the National Geographic Channel. In the show, Millan helps people work with challenging dogs.

The Dog Whisperer *soon became one of the National Geographic Channel's most popular shows.*

CESAR'S WAY

Some people disagreed with Millan's methods. Millan believes most dogs are given too much affection. Instead they need more exercise and **discipline**. Many veterinarians believe Millan's ideas are unscientific. But Millan believes his ways are safe and work well.

Millan thinks pet owners must act like dog pack leaders.

SAVING DOGS

In 2007, Millan started the Cesar Millan **Foundation**. The foundation helps shelter dogs find homes. It supports the **sterilizing** of dogs. And it also teaches children how to safely work with dogs. In 2015, Millan renamed the foundation the PACK (People in Action for **Canines** and Kindness) Project.

In 2010, the Cesar Millan Foundation held a huge walk. It raised money for homeless pets.

Millan visits animal shelters all across the country.

CHANGES FOR MILLAN

Millan continued to reach more and more dog owners. He published his first book, *Cesar's Way*, in 2006. It became a best seller. Three years later, the DPC moved to the hills of Santa Clarita, California. The new property gave Millan more room to exercise dogs.

In 2007, Cesar published his second book, Be the Pack Leader.

Millan's DPC rests on 43 acres (17 ha) of land. It has many walking trails and a swimming pool for dogs!

A HOME
FOR EVERY DOG

The Dog Whisperer ended in 2012. But in 2014, Millan began the dog training show *Cesar 911*. Meanwhile, he travels the world teaching his methods. Millan also runs an advice website for dog owners. He continues working to help dogs have safe and happy homes.

Cesar with his dog Junior

MORE ABOUT MILLAN

Millan became a US CITIZEN in 2009.

In 2015, Millan and his son Calvin began starring in the NICK JR. TV show *Mutt and Stuff*. The show is about a school for dogs. It uses real dogs and puppets.

Millan's pit bull JUNIOR helps him work with other dogs. Junior's calm presence helps other dogs relax.

Millan has written SIX BOOKS about dogs and dog training.

TEST YOUR KNOWLEDGE

1. What job did Millan dream of having when he was a child?

2. What was the name of Millan's first TV show?

3. Millan believes most dogs need more affection. True or false?

THINK ABOUT IT!

Do you have any pets? How do you train them?

ANSWERS: 1. Dog trainer 2. The Dog Whisperer 3. False

GLOSSARY

behaviorist – someone who studies the way a person or animal acts.

canine – of or relating to dogs.

discipline – training that molds, corrects, or perfects something.

foundation – an organization that is created to do something that helps society.

groomer – someone who takes care of an animal's fur, nails, claws, or hooves.

psychology – the science of the mind and behavior.

sterilize – to make a person or animal unable to produce offspring.